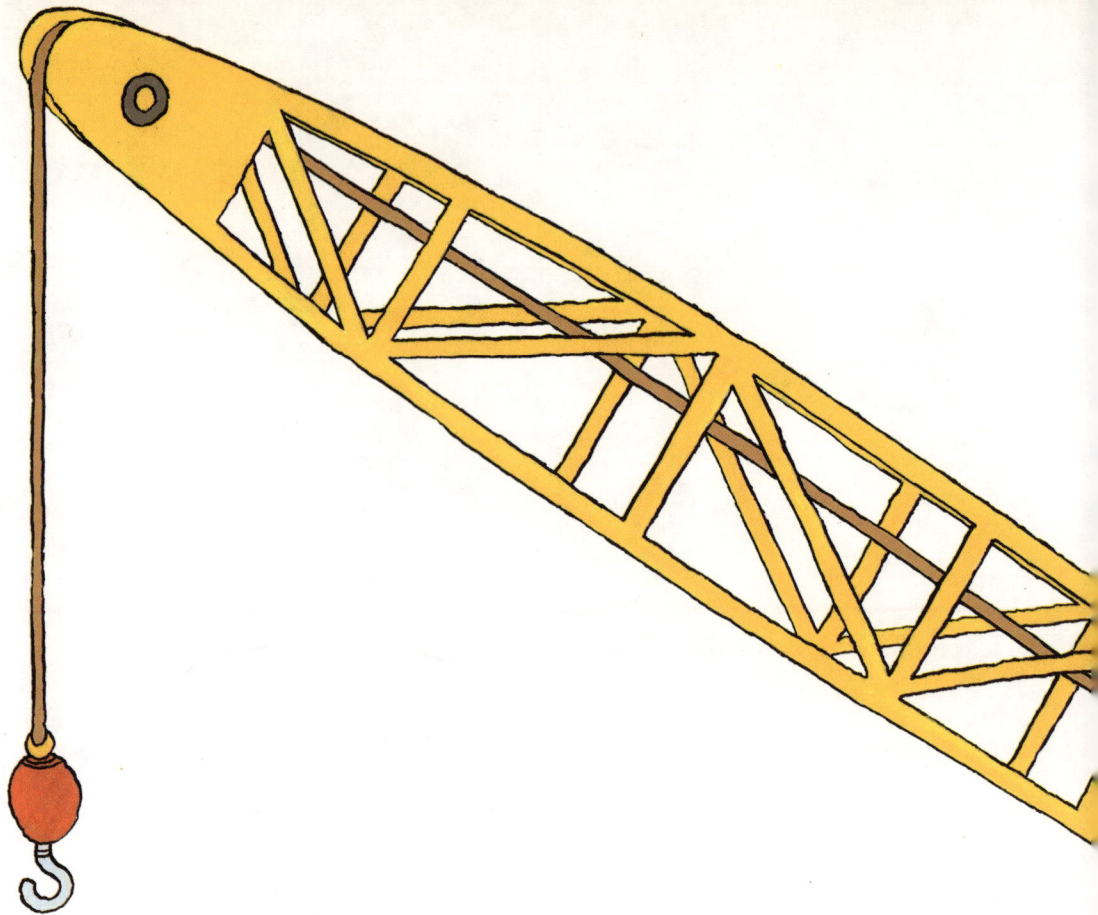

Copyright © 1986 by Tony Wells.

All rights reserved. First published in
the United States in 1986 by Platt & Munk,
a division of Grosset & Dunlap.
Grosset & Dunlap is a member of
The Putnam Publishing Group, New York.
Originally published in Great Britain in 1986
by Walker Books Ltd., London.

Printed in Italy.

Library of Congress Catalog Card Number:86-80518
ISBN 0-448-10828-3 A B C D E F G H I J

My First Book of
MACHINES

illustrated by
Tony Wells

Platt & Munk, Publishers • New York
A Division of Grosset & Dunlap

CONTENTS

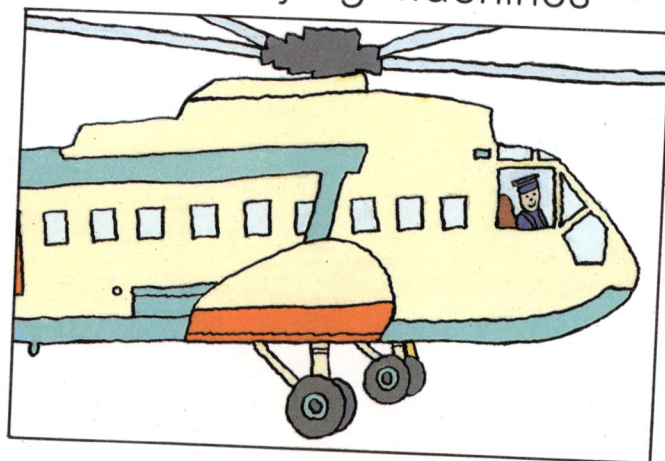

18-19 Machines at Sea

20-21 The Garage

22-23 Toys That Go

24-25 Space Machines

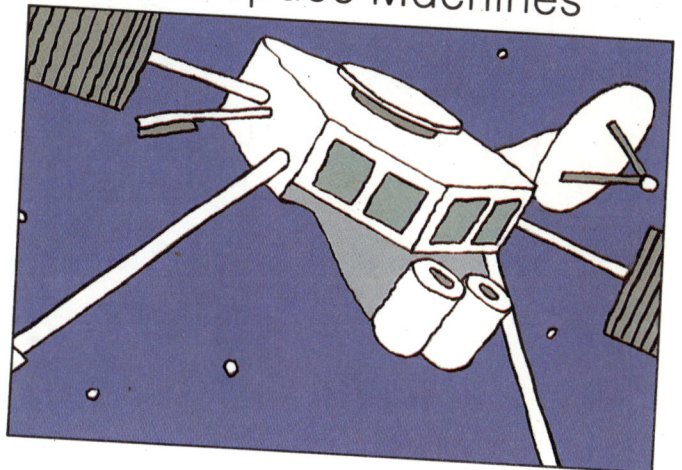

26-27 Machines Old and New

28-29 Silly Machines

Machines at Home

washing machine

toaster

kettle

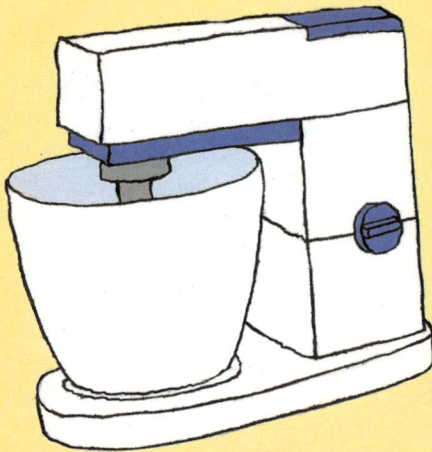
mixer

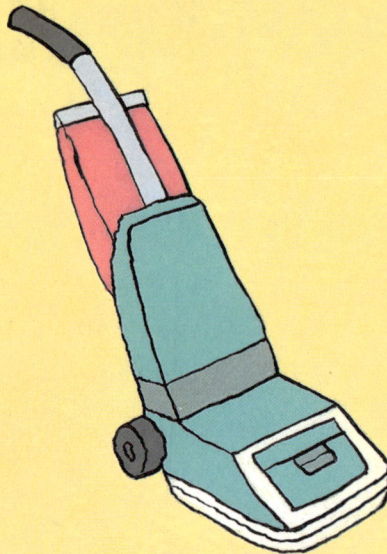
vacuum cleaner

iron

electric drill

clock

stove

Can you find the machines in this picture?

Message Machines

radio

computer

binoculars

telephone

typewriter

record player

camera

headphones

television

cassette
player

Machines on Wheels

car carrier

go-cart

car

bus

crane

motorcycle

van

tanker

Farm Machines

combine

plow   tractor

trailer

pickup truck

Flying Machines

cargo plane

passenger plane

balloon

blimp

helicopter

jet

Machines for Building

backhoe

cement mixer

jack-hammer

dumper

paving truck

bulldozer

crane

Can you name the machines?

Machines at Sea

tanker

hover craft

yacht

lightship

ocean liner    trawler    tugboat    motor-boat

The Garage

work
light

dashboard

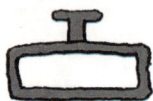

rear view
mirror

steering
wheel

wrench

gas pump

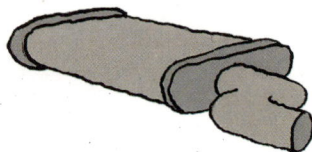

muffler

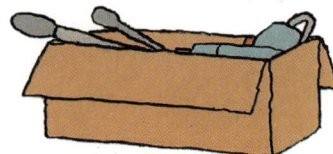

tool box

Can you find these things in the picture?

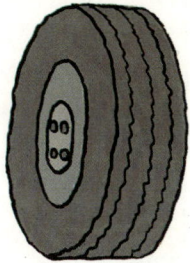
tire

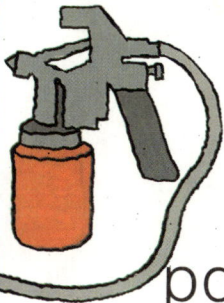
paint sprayer

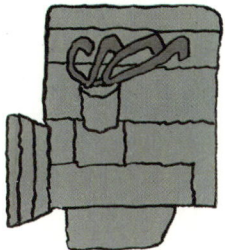
engine

gear shift

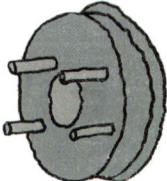
wheel hub

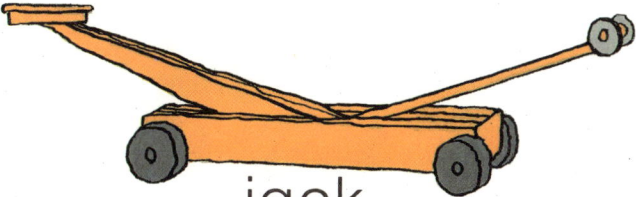
jack

hammer

Toys That Go

robot

wind-up duck

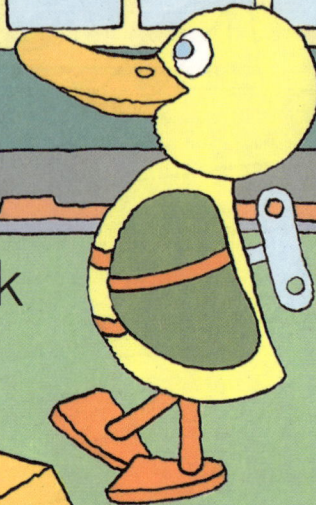

wind-up crane

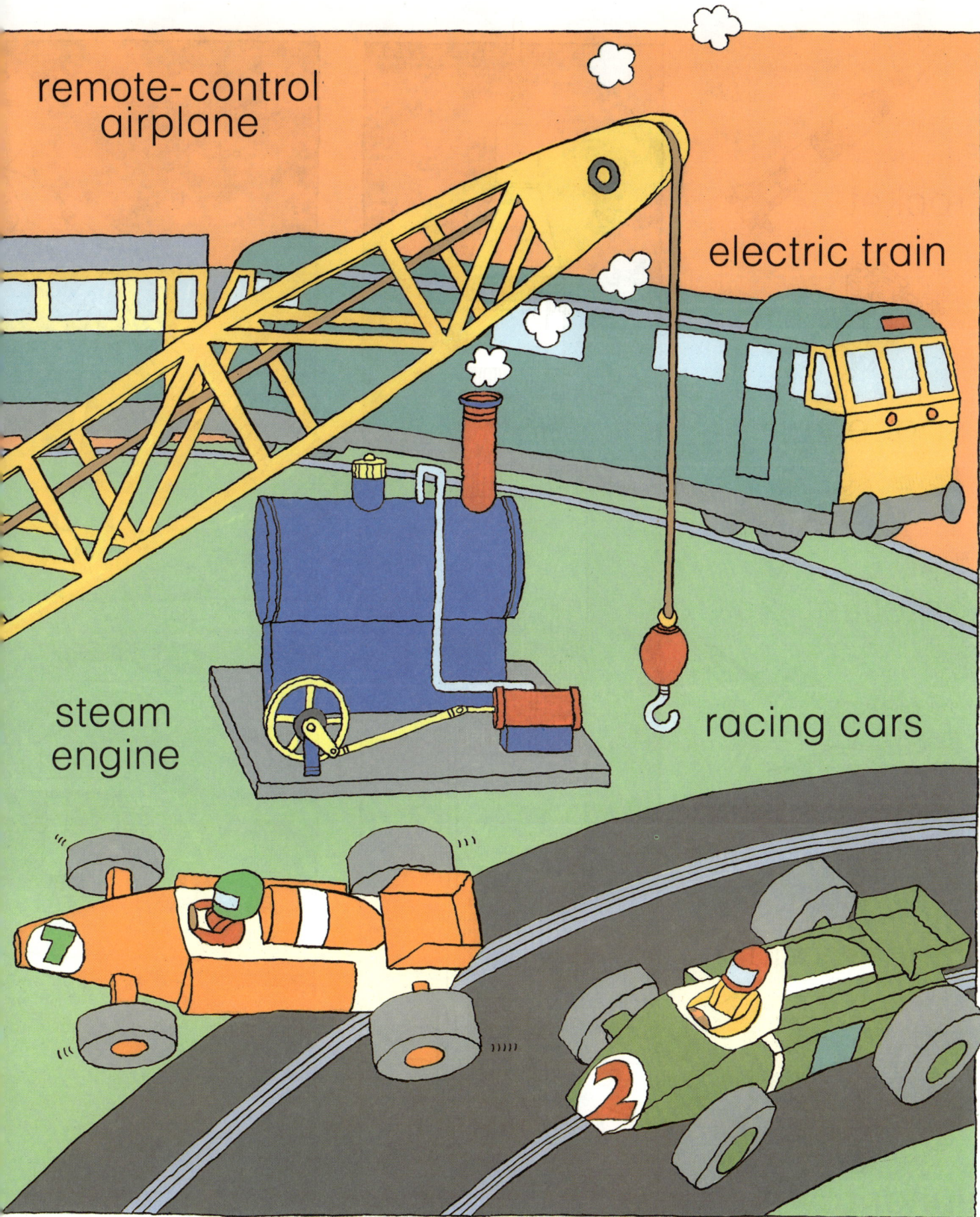

remote-control
airplane

electric train

steam
engine

racing cars

Space Machines

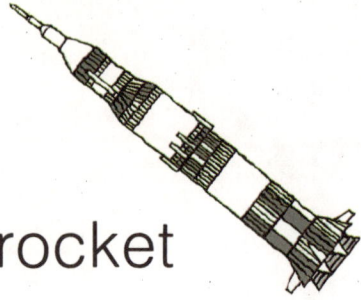

rocket

space suit

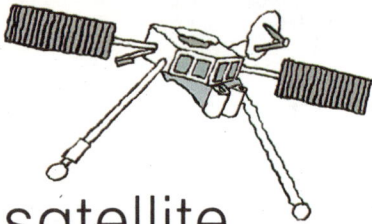

satellite

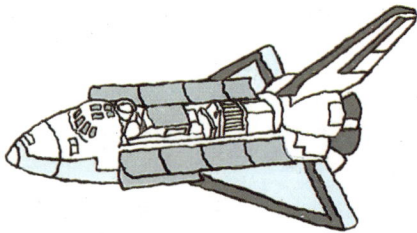

space shuttle

lunar module

lunar rover

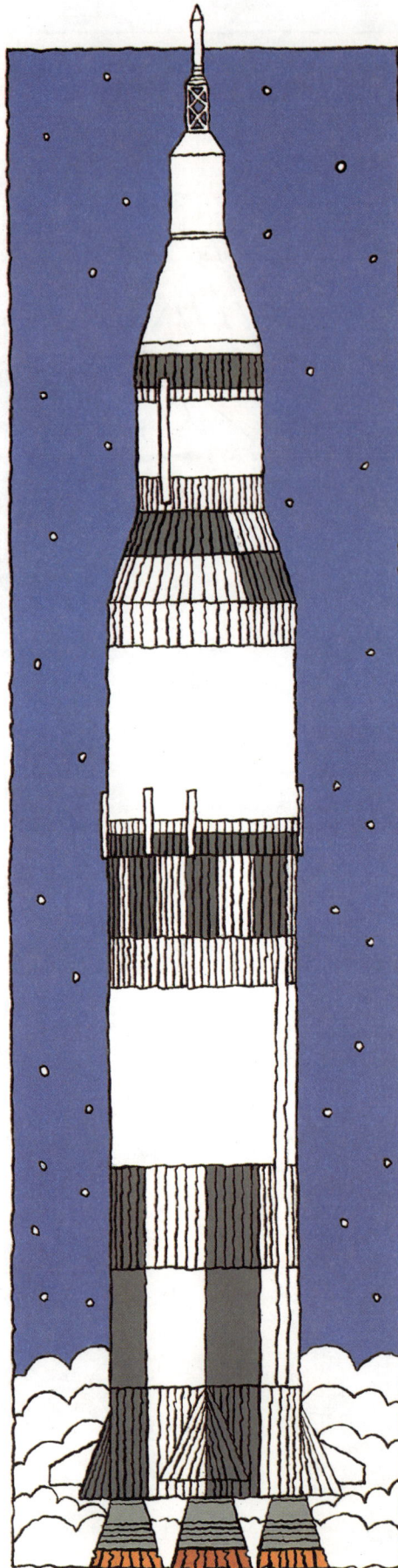

Machines Old and New

Which machines are old and which are new?

radios

cameras

racing cars

airplanes

bicycles

trains

Silly Machines
What is wrong in each of these pictures?

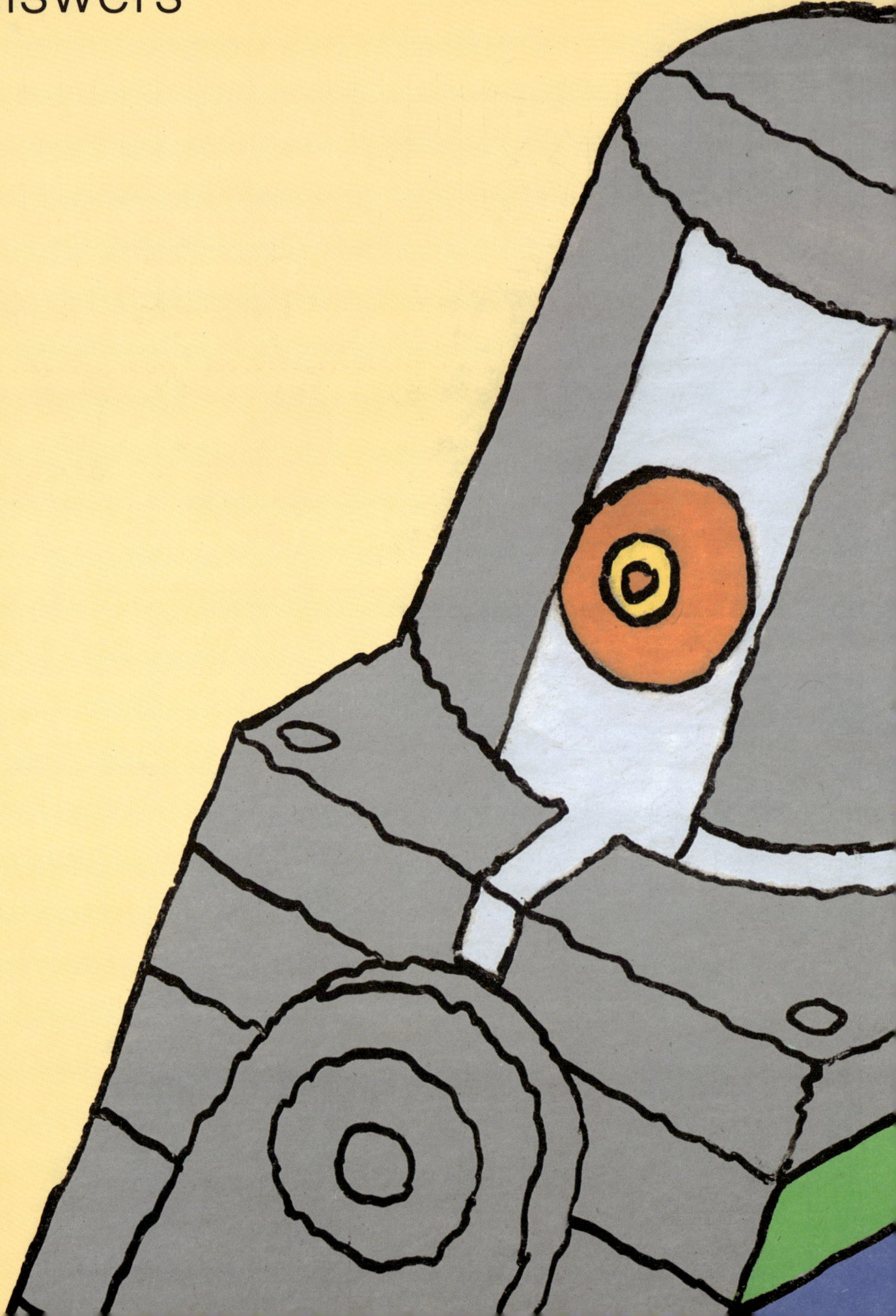

Answers

26-27
Machines Old and New
- In each picture the machine on the left is old and the machine on the right is new.

28-29
Silly Machines
- The car is flying, and the steering wheels are on the wrong sides.
- The kettle is ironing.
- The vacuum cleaner is mowing the grass.
- The cement mixer is doing the laundry.